T0061709

— How to —
DRINK COFFEE

For Peter and Peter

First published in the United Kingdom in 2023
by Skittledog, an imprint of Thames & Hudson Ltd,
181A High Holborn, London WC1V 7QX

Concept and layout © Thames & Hudson 2023
Text © Sarah Ford 2023
Illustrations © Clare Owen 2023

All Rights Reserved. No part of this publication may be
reproduced or transmitted in any form or by any means,
electronic or mechanical, including photocopy, recording
or any other information storage and retrieval system,
without prior permission in writing from the publisher.

British Library Catalog-in-Publication Data
A catalog record for this book is available from
the British Library

ISBN 978-1-837-76025-1

Printed and bound in China by C&C Printing Offset Co., Ltd

MIX
Paper | Supporting
responsible forestry
FSC
www.fsc.org   FSC® C008047

Senior Editor: Jodi Simpson
Designer: Masumi Briozzo
Production: Felicity Awdry

Be the first to know about our new releases,
exclusive content and author events by visiting
skittledog.com
thamesandhudson.com
thamesandhudsonusa.com
thamesandhudson.com.au

How to —

DRINK COFFEE

SARAH FORD

Skittledog

Contents

A Rich History

It is hard to imagine all that goes into producing your morning coffee. The humble coffee bean has been traveling around the world for hundreds of years, and there is a rich history of stories about how beans have been exported, traded, smuggled, and stolen. Coffee was supposedly discovered in Ethiopia in 700 CE. It is said that a goatherd noticed his goats were dancing around strangely after eating red berries that they had found on the ground. He sampled the fruit from the nearby evergreen bushes for himself and felt ecstatic. Rumor has it that the herder shared his findings with a monk, who ate the fruits to help him stay up at night and pray.

There is little doubt that the stimulation provided by coffee has a big part to play in its enduring popularity. In fact, the coffeehouse came into being in the Ottoman Empire, where coffee was considered to be the best alternative to alcohol, which was banned. The coffeehouse was also a place to gather, talk, share ideas, and socialize. Political sentiments often developed there, which lead to coffeehouses being banned when political rule was challenged. Coffeehouses were found in Vienna, Damascus, and Constantinople by the 1500s. At this time, coffee was often sweetened to make it more palatable. By the 17th century, coffee, tea, and chocolate were all popular in England, where the first coffeehouse had opened in 1652. Demand grew, with many more opening and playing a part in English society.

Coffee has come a long way since then. Today, the taste is exceptional, with many growers, producers, and varieties to choose from. All the processes that go into producing the drink we know and love have been finely honed, and growers produce specialty varieties and blends all around the world. However you drink it, one thing remains constant: the delight that a good cup of coffee can bring. But it's not just for drinking –coffee can take cakes, cookies, and even savory food to new levels of deliciousness.

From Bush to Bean to Cup

The coffee beans we know and love are the seeds of a coffee cherry, so called because they are a bright red when they are ripe and ready to be picked. The cherries grow on a bush or tree, which can take three to four years to start producing fruit. The fruit is harvested once or twice a year, usually by hand, and needs to be processed quickly.

First, the seeds—which become the coffee beans—are removed from the pulp of the fruit and placed in water tanks to ferment for up to 36 hours. After this, they are washed to remove any remaining pulp and then spread out to dry in the sun. A more traditional method involves drying the whole cherries in the sun, periodically raking and turning them over, and covering them at night; it can take several weeks for all the moisture to dry out. The beans must then be hulled to remove the outer layers of the fruit. They are then sorted by size and weight and any defective beans are removed. These beans, called "green coffee," are exported in jute bags by ship.

Taste and roasting

Coffee is tasted many times in a process known as cupping. The beans are looked at to check their quality, then they are roasted in a laboratory, ground up and infused with boiling water. The aroma of the coffee is "nosed," a spoonful is slurped with a view to covering all the taste buds and the tongue, then the coffee is spat out. The tasters describe the sweetness, acidity, balance, and flavor of the coffee.

The roasting process changes the green coffee into the brown beans that we buy. The beans are roasted in machines set to 550°F and are kept moving to avoid burning. When they turn brown, they release an aromatic oil.

Recipe Notes

This book includes recipes made with nuts and nut derivatives. Anyone who has allergic reactions to nut or nut derivatives, or who is vulnerable to allergies, is advised to avoid dishes made with them.

Standard level spoon measurements are used:
1 tablespoon = 15ml
1 dessertspoon = 10ml
1 teaspoon = 5ml

Espresso: 1 shot = 1½ teaspoons (7g) ground coffee / 2 tablespoons (30ml) espresso.

Alcohol: 1 measure = 2 tablespoons (30ml).

For reliable results in the baking recipes, use the weight measurements supplied rather than the cup measurements.

Ovens should be preheated to the specified temperature. For fan ovens, follow the manufacturer's instructions to adjust the time and temperature.

Coffee Origin and Taste

The Americas
The majority of the world's coffee is supplied by the Americas. From Brazil to Guatemala, there is a wide range of beans, often characterized as smooth and sweet, well balanced with a bright acidity and a crisp and clean taste. The aroma of these coffees is often described as pure, with notes of chocolate, nuts, fruits, and spices. Some of the most expensive coffees come from Central America. One of the reasons that these coffees are so popular is that they are consistently balanced. There is great variety and quality.

The Caribbean
Caribbean beans are known for their balance and mildly acidic flavor. They are uncomplicated, rich, and smooth with notes of wine and smoke. The coffees are soft and almost creamy but tend to lack intense top notes. While clean and pleasant to drink, they are not particularly complex.

Asia

Asian coffees are not as popular as their counterparts in Africa and South America. That said, there are some that think Pacific coffee has a lot to offer. Asian coffees vary, but they tend to be full bodied with earthy, woody notes. They have a mild acidity but can be slightly bitter with a salty aftertaste. Coffees from Southeast Asia tend to be either loved or hated.

Africa

Ethiopia is the birthplace of coffee, and Africa is thought to have some of the best beans in the world. Central and Eastern Africa grow and export large amounts of coffee. Each country has different techniques, making its coffees unique. African coffee is often known for its floral, fruity, and berry notes and complex flavors. The acidity is bright, and there are hints of citrus and jasmine florals. African coffee is very diverse, with many varieties grown across the continent.

Know Your Beans

There are four main types of coffee bean: Arabica, Robusta, Liberica, and Excelsa. They each have their own unique taste profile.

Arabica

This is the best-known and most popular coffee bean, the most commonly produced, and the best quality. Arabica beans are grown at high altitudes and need shade and steady rain. The plants are easy to look after, aromatic, and flavorsome—hence their popularity.

Robusta

The second most produced, Robusta beans are resilient and hardy, and therefore easy to produce. The beans are grown in hot climates and need less rain than Arabica. They are high in caffeine but have a sharper flavor, often described as chocolaty.

Liberica

Liberica beans are less common, irregular in shape, and larger. They grow on tall trees and are harvested by pickers on ladders. The flavor of the beans is described as smoky, floral, and fruity, with a unique aroma.

Excelsa

These beans have recently been reclassified as members of the Liberica family, but they taste very different. The small, round beans have complex flavors of berries with chocolate notes.

Know Your Coffee

Ristretto

Espresso

Lungo
espresso

Macchiato

Cortado

Cappuccino

Latte

Flat white

Mocha

Americano

Affogato

Steamy

If there is a better way to start your day than with coffee, I don't know what it is. Whether you take your coffee short and dark or long and creamy, the aroma will lift your senses, the mug will warm your hands and the taste will enliven your body. Coffee can kick-start a good day or make a bad one more bearable.

How to Choose the Right Milk

Milk can make all the difference to a cup of coffee. There are many different kinds of milk available and different ways to use them, depending on what kind of coffee you're preparing.

What is the best milk to use?

The milk you use is entirely up to you and your personal taste, but some types of milk naturally lend themselves better to coffee than others. Cappuccinos and lattes are best made with full-fat or whole milk, as they contain protein and fat that helps with the flavor and foam. A coffee made with skim or nonfat milk has a more intense flavor but one that won't last as long. Oat milk is considered to be the best nondairy alternative, especially the barista editions, as it is flavorsome and it froths and steams well. Soy milk is best avoided as it is difficult to froth and has a tendency to curdle.

Air and heat

To turn your everyday chilled milk into something silky, velvety, and creamy, you simply have to introduce air into it and heat it—this is called stretching the milk. It can be done easily at home and the milk can then be used in different ways to transform your coffee: scoop it on top of a cappuccino or whip it into a latte.

Froth or steam?

Steamed milk is hot milk that produces a delicate foam. Adding steam aerates and heats the milk. This is often done with a steaming wand, though it can be done successfully at home without a wand (see page 18). It makes the milk hot and frothy by breaking down the fat into tiny air bubbles known as microfoam. Steamed milk has a heavier, smoother texture than frothed milk and can be used in many coffee drinks.

Frothed milk is made by aerating the milk to add air bubbles and create a frothy, lighter texture (see page 19). The technique produces larger bubbles that hold their shape to create foam. Frothed milk tends to be used in foam-filled beverages such as cappuccinos. It should be airy to drink and can be used hot or cold.

Mastering the Perfect Pour

With your steamed milk (see page 18) in a pitcher, tap the pitcher on a countertop and give the milk a swirl to remove large air bubbles. The milk should have a velvety sheen and texture. The pouring technique is important: aim to pour the milk directly into the middle of the cup, then in a circular motion out to the edge of the cup. Hold back the foam with a spoon and then spoon the foam onto the top of your drink. Different drinks will need different amounts of milk and foam (see page 26).

How to Steam Milk

If you like your coffee with steamed milk, there are a few different ways you can prepare it. The perfect milk temperature is 150°F. For best results, use a food thermometer to check the temperature of the milk as you're heating it so you can stop the process at the perfect time and avoid scalding.

In the microwave

Fill ⅓ of a mug with the milk of your choice and heat in the microwave for about 30 seconds. You may have to experiment to determine the exact amount of time needed. If need be, microwave for a further 10 seconds, or until you have the right temperature.

On the stovetop

If you heat the milk in a pan on the stovetop, you will have more control over the heat. Milk can scald easily, so warm it over low to medium heat, stirring regularly. This can take 1-3 minutes.

Using the frothing wand on an espresso machine

Fill a metal pitcher to the bottom of the wand's spout with your chilled milk of choice. Make sure the steam wand is clean and at the correct temperature. Place the wand just under the surface of the milk. This heats the milk and creates a small whirlpool. After 5-10 seconds, immerse the wand further. Keep steaming until the temperature reaches 150°F— the pitcher should be almost too hot to touch.

How to Froth Milk

Immersion blender

Stovetop frother

Handheld electric frother

French press frother

No-Frills Frothing

Pour your chosen chilled milk into a large microwaveable jar or bottle with a sealed lid, so that it is ⅓ full (or contains your desired amount). Shake the milk vigorously until it doubles in size and is frothy—this can take up to 1 minute. Remove the lid and microwave the milk for 30 seconds. This will set the foam. You will need to watch to make sure that the milk doesn't overflow. If this happens, pause the process to allow the milk to settle, then start again. If the milk is not hot enough, microwave for a further 10 seconds or until you reach the desired heat.

How to Brew Coffee

Great coffee starts with the right equipment and the right beans.

Grinder

Coffee tastes best when it is freshly ground. If you grind beans as you need them, you will ensure you get the best flavor. An electric grinder is by far the easiest and most efficient way to grind beans, although you can also grind by hand. Coffee can be very fine, fine, medium, or coarse ground according to how you intend to make your coffee (see page 21).

Scale

For weighing beans and grounds.

Kettle

A normal kettle is fine, but if you want to move to the next level you could invest in a pour-over kettle with a thermometer.

Filter papers

When buying filter papers check that you buy the right ones for the equipment you have. Each manufacturer will recommend a paper for their product. These are generally used for pour-over coffees.

Coffee beans

It is important to take your time to find the right coffee for you. Do you like the chocolaty tones of Brazilian coffee or the vibrant citrus flavors of Kenyan coffee? The best way to find out is to try different types, read reviews, attend tasting sessions, and experiment in coffeehouses. There are also many experts to be found in independent coffeehouses who will be pleased to share their knowledge.

The right grind

To get the best coffee, it is important to have the right grind for your brew method.

- Turkish—extra fine
- Espresso—fine
- Aeropress—medium fine
- Pour over—medium
- Home espresso machine—medium coarse
- French press—coarse
- Cold brew—extra coarse

The right water temperature

Your water should be 190-200°F, or just below the boiling point. If you boil the kettle, let it cool a little before pouring.

Making Coffee in a French Press

- 1 rounded tbsp (18g) coffee; 1¼ cups (300ml) water = coffee for 1
- 2 rounded tbsp (30g) coffee; 2 cups (475ml) water = coffee for 2
- 4 rounded tbsp (60g) coffee; 4¼ cups (1 litre) water = coffee for 4

Brewing Methods

Everyone has their favorite coffee-brewing method. Here are the more common ones.

French press

This is a simple and quick way to make as many cups as you want by steeping medium-coarse ground coffee. Add the right amount of coffee for the number of cups you want to brew (see page 21), pour in the hot water (190-200°F) and allow it to steep for 3-4 minutes, then press down and serve.

Moka pot

A traditional stovetop brewing method from Italy that moves boiling water through coffee grounds in cycles. To use the pot, fill the bottom chamber to just below the valve with water preheated to around 160°F. Fill the filter with medium ground coffee—level it off but don't pack it down. Screw the top and bottom chambers together and place the pot on the stovetop over a high heat. When you hear the coffee bubbling, turn the heat off. Any residual heat will push enough water through to brew all the rest of the coffee. The process can take up to 10 minutes.

Pour over

This method brews the coffee straight into your mug through a filter paper. Place the pour-over brewer on top of your mug and add the filter. Add 1 tablespoon of medium ground coffee to the filter paper and pour 1¼ cups (300ml) of boiled and slightly cooled water over the top of the grounds. The brewed coffee will drip through into the mug.

Chemex

The Chemex operates in a similar way to a pour-over brewer, but brews the coffee into a carafe instead of a mug, allowing you to make more than one cup at a time. You will need a thicker filter and medium-coarse ground coffee.

Espresso machine

These machines can be expensive, but they are an investment and well worthwhile if you are a coffee lover—if you use your machine daily, it will soon become worth the outlay. Espresso machines work by pushing pressurized hot water through tightly packed grounds in a filter. They often come with a built-in milk steamer. The downside to the machines is the cleaning and descaling they require, but many consider the effort worth it for a great shot of espresso. Each machine comes with an individual set of operating instructions.

Aeropress

This is a handheld, portable, manual coffee maker for one person. It works similarly to a syringe, with a plunger inserted into an outer tube. Ground filter or espresso coffee and boiled water are added to the tube. Once the grounds have steeped, the plunger forces them through a filter to produce concentrated, espresso-style coffee. An aeropress can also be used for filter or cold-brew coffee.

How to Make Espresso Without a Machine

If you don't want an expensive, bulky espresso machine, a moka pot or French press could be perfect for you.

A moka pot works in the same way as an espresso machine by forcing steam and boiling water through ground coffee and produces coffee very similar to an espresso.

Use 1 tablespoon of medium ground, espresso-roasted coffee and ¾ cup (175ml) of water and follow the instructions on page 22.

You can also make espresso in a French press. Finely grind 2 tablespoons of espresso-roasted beans and warm your press. Add the coffee and a cup of boiled and slightly cooled water. Allow the coffee to steep, then gently stir. Add the filter, let the coffee brew for about 3 minutes, then press down slowly and pour a double or two single espressos.

The brew ratio

This is the ratio of coffee to water. Each different coffee will have a different brew ratio. A good starting point for an espresso is a ratio of 1:2– 1 part coffee to 2 parts water. The final weight of the coffee drink should be twice the weight of the ground coffee. This ratio can be altered if your preference is for a smaller, stronger espresso like those typically made in Italy.

Crema

Crema—the creamy brown foam on top of the coffee—is possibly the most important part of espresso. It is created when slightly cooled boiled water emulsifies the oil in coffee. Traditionally, espresso was only considered good if it had a decent topping of crema, though some people find that it makes the coffee too bitter and scrape it off before drinking.

Espresso explained

• **Espresso**—a small, dark, intense drink, 2 tablespoons (30ml), made with finely ground coffee in a brew ratio of 1:2, with a small head of crema on top. A double espresso is 4 tablespoons (60ml) and is known as a doppio espresso.

• **Ristretto**—a smaller, stronger "restricted" espresso, 1½ tablespoons (22ml), made with finely ground coffee and less water than espresso.

• **Lungo**—a longer espresso, 4 tablespoons (60ml), made with two or three times the amount of water as traditional espresso and a coarse-ground, lighter-roast coffee.

Demitasse

An espresso cup is known as a *demitasse*, from the French meaning "half cup." It measures 4-6 tablespoons (60-90ml)—a little cup that holds a great deal of flavor and punches well above its weight.

Coffees with an Espresso Base

Macchiato

A macchiato–from the Italian for "stained" or "marked"–is an espresso with a spot of milk added to it, just enough to slightly lighten or "stain" the dark color of the coffee. In coffeehouses it is often served topped with a little foam.

Latte

The latte, a light and milky coffee topped with froth, was developed for customers who found espresso too bitter and wanted a longer, less intense drink. If you like a milky coffee, this is the one for you. It is made with a single shot of espresso mixed with steamed milk and topped with frothed milk. It has more milk and a milder flavor than a cappuccino.

Cappuccino

The cappuccino is a layered coffee consisting of a double shot of espresso with the same amount of steamed milk and topped with foam. There should be a 1:1 ratio of liquid to foam. Dating back to the 19th century, the drink was named after Capuchin friars, who wore robes of the same color.

Flat white

Hailing from Australasia, the flat white has been adopted all over the world. It is a smaller version of the latte, with 2 shots of espresso and a stronger coffee to milk ratio of 1:2, with just a touch of foam. It has the perfect topping for coffee art (see page 28).

Cortado

A Spanish coffee, served in a glass. A shot (2 tablespoons/30ml) of espresso is combined with 2 tablespoons (30ml) of steamed milk, making a small coffee with good flavor and no foam.

Americano

After World War 2, American soldiers based in Italy found that the espresso they were served was too strong for them—they wanted their coffee to resemble the filter coffee they drank at home and requested extra water with their espresso to dilute the taste. This coffee became known as *caffè americano*—"American coffee." Nowadays it is known as café Americano or just Americano. To make this at home, add slightly cooled boiled water to a cup and pour a double shot of espresso over the top. If the coffee is still too bitter, try scraping the crema off the top. Serve with milk on the side, if you like.

Should You Sprinkle Chocolate on a Cappuccino?

The short answer to this is that you can make your cappuccino however you like—use oat milk, add syrup, or sprinkle the top with chocolate or cinnamon. It really is down to personal taste, though cappuccino in its true, original form does not have chocolate on the top.

Latte Art

If you go to an independent coffeehouse, you may find the barista has adorned the top of your coffee with a beautiful work of art. Latte art is like the frosting on a cake—a final flourish that lifts your coffee and brings joy. It shows that the barista is a craftsperson and that they have taken care with the preparation of your drink. From hearts to tulips to smiley faces, latte art is no mean feat: it requires perfectly frothed milk, great timing, a steady hand, and perfect positioning. Practice makes perfect, so start simple and build up to creating masterpieces in your coffee at home.

The heart

Steam your milk (see page 18) and make sure you have plenty of foam, then add it to a pitcher. Pour your espresso into a coffee cup, then tilt the cup toward the pitcher of steamed milk. Add the milk to the tilted cup, pouring slowly in circles until the cup is half full and trying to keep the crema on the surface of the drink; hold the foam back with a spoon. Slowly place the cup on a flat surface. Move the pitcher so that it is right above the surface of the coffee and keep pouring so that the foam forms a blob on the surface of the coffee. Remember, it is the pitcher and milk that are moving and not the cup. When the cup is almost full, pour the milk in a line through the middle of the blob to the other side to create a heart shape. Present to someone you love.

Gingerbread Latte Like Christmas in a glass!

MAKES 2 MUGS
OR GLASSES

- 1 tablespoon ginger syrup
  (see page 60)
- 3 shots espresso
- 1¼ cups (300ml) whole
  milk or oat milk
- whipped cream, to top
- crushed gingersnap and
  cinnamon, for sprinkling
  (optional)

While you are brewing your espresso, warm the milk in a small saucepan on the stovetop until simmering. Turn off the heat and whisk the milk until light and frothy. Add the espresso and syrup to a tall heat-safe glass, then add your frothy milk and stir gently. Top with whipped cream, crushed gingersnap, and cinnamon.

Coffee Mocha Warming and sweet, this drink is perfect for winter.

MAKES 1 MUG

- 1½ tablespoons semi-
  sweet chocolate, chopped
- 2 teaspoons hot
  chocolate powder
- 2 shots espresso
- hot milk, to top up
  whipped cream and mini
  marshmallows, to decorate
  (optional)

Place the chocolate in a mug and melt it slowly in a microwave, then stir well. Add the hot chocolate powder and espresso to the melted chocolate and stir thoroughly. Top up with hot milk. Decorate with whipped cream and marshmallows, if you like.

Pumpkin-Spice Latte A coffee drink full of traditional fall flavors.

MAKES 1 MUG
OR GLASS

- 2 shots espresso
- 1¼ cups (300ml) whole
  milk or oat milk
- 2 tablespoons pumpkin
  puree, homemade
  (see page 33) or tinned
- 2 heaping teaspoons
  brown sugar
- 1 teaspoon Pumpkin
  Spice (see below)
- dash of vanilla extract

While you are brewing the espresso, warm the milk in a small saucepan on the stovetop until simmering. Turn off the heat and whisk the milk until light and frothy. Add the puree, sugar, spice, and vanilla to a long heat-safe glass and stir. Then add the espresso, stir again, and add the frothy milk. Stir gently but well to mix.

Pumpkin Spice Add to Pumpkin-Spice Lattes and other coffee drinks for a taste of fall.

MAKES ENOUGH FOR
ABOUT 25 DRINKS

- 1½ tablespoons
  ground cinnamon
- 2 teaspoons
  ground ginger
- ½ teaspoon
  ground nutmeg
- ¼ teaspoon
  ground cloves

Mix all the spices together and store in a sealed jar.

Pumpkin Puree You can make your own puree quite easily if you can't get hold of the tinned variety. Heat the oven to 400°F. Cut a pumpkin in half and remove the seeds. Place the halves flat side down on a roasting pan and roast for 40–60 minutes, depending on size. Once cooled, scrape out the flesh and blitz in a blender until smooth.

Top 5 Things to Dunk in Coffee

- **Biscotti** (see page 86): Designed by the Italians with dunking in mind.
- **Shortbread:** It won't fall apart and will melt in your mouth, not your coffee.
- **Almond horns**: The perfect shape and strength for dunking.
- **Doughnuts**: They're not called Dunkin' Donuts for nothing.
- **Gingerbread men**: Head first, hold on tight to the feet!

INTERNATIONAL COFFEE TRADITIONS

North Scandinavian *kaffeost* is prepared by adding cubes of Finnish cheese, made from reindeer milk, to a cup and pouring hot black coffee over the top. It is rich, smoky, and buttery, and best served with a spoon, as the cheese does not melt but rather absorbs the coffee.

Brazil's *cafezinho* is like an espresso but stronger. It is dense, black, and very sweet, and a traditional part of local hospitality.

In **Turkey** it is customary to serve coffee with a glass of water. A sip of water is taken to clear the palate so it is ready to experience the full taste of the strong, sweet, black coffee. Coffee is served to the oldest person in the room first, as a sign of respect. It is accompanied by a sweet treat, such as Turkish delight.

Coffee in the **Middle East** is all about hospitality, with the first drink offered to a guest. Rich in flavor and with added spices, the coffee is served black, often with dried dates for sweetness.

In **Vietnam**, the locals like their coffee strong and bitter, but with the added sweetness of condensed milk. It is usually made in a French press and can be served hot or cold.

In **Malaysia**, the locals drink a blend of coffee and tea known as *yuanyang*, with a ratio of 3 parts black coffee to 7 parts milky tea. It is served hot or cold.

Irish Coffee The perfect end to dinner.

MAKES 1 TALL GLASS

– ⅔ cup (150ml) strong-
  brewed coffee
– 2 measures Irish whiskey
– 1 teaspoon brown sugar
– 2 tablespoons
  heavy cream
– pinch of nutmeg,
  to decorate

Pour the coffee into a heat-safe glass, add
the whiskey and sugar, and gently stir to mix.
Gently pour the cream over the back of a spoon
onto the surface of the coffee so that it forms a
creamy layer. Decorate with a pinch of nutmeg.

Calypso Coffee This drink is similar to an
Irish coffee but has the taste of the Caribbean with
dark rum and sugar.

MAKES 1 TALL GLASS

– ⅔ cup (150ml) strong-
  brewed coffee
– 1 measure coffee liqueur
– 1 measure dark rum
– 1 teaspoon brown sugar
– 2 tablespoons
  heavy cream

Pour the coffee into a heat-safe glass, add the
liqueur, rum, and sugar, and gently stir to mix.
Gently pour the cream over the back of a spoon
onto the surface of the coffee so that it forms a
creamy layer.

French Coffee
An orange kick makes this coffee sweet and delicious.

MAKES 1 TALL GLASS

- ⅔ cup (150ml) strong-brewed coffee
- 1 measure coffee liqueur
- 1 measure orange liqueur
- 1 teaspoon brown sugar
- whipped cream and grated chocolate, to decorate

Pour the coffee into a heat-safe glass, add the liqueurs and sugar, and gently stir to mix. Top with whipped cream and the chocolate.

Hot White Russian
This hot version of the classic cocktail is a great winter warmer.

MAKES 1 SHORT GLASS

- 1 measure vodka
- 1 measure coffee liqueur
- 1 shot espresso
- 4 tablespoons steamed oat milk or cream, frothed, to top up

Pour the vodka and coffee liqueur into a short heat-safe glass, add the espresso, then top up with the steamed milk or cream.

Mexican Coffee
Chili complements coffee, chocolate, and cinnamon flavors.

MAKES 1 GLASS

- 1½ tablespoons semi-sweet chocolate, chopped
- 1 pinch cinnamon
- 1 pinch chili powder
- 2 shots espresso
- 1 measure dark coffee liqueur
- 1 measure white tequila
- whipped cream and grated chocolate, to decorate (optional)

Gently melt the chocolate in a saucepan over low heat. Add the spices and espresso to the melted chocolate and stir thoroughly. Take the saucepan off the heat and add the liqueur and tequila. Stir well and pour into a heat-safe glass. Decorate with whipped cream and grated chocolate, if you like.

Chilled

Hot days are made for chilled coffees. Sit back and relax with one of these delicious recipes—simple but impressive to make for yourself or for guests. If you're having a party, the chilled cocktails are guaranteed to get things going.

Coffee Lassi
A sweet and creamy yogurt drink that is lovely with breakfast.

MAKES 2 GLASSES

MAKES 2 GLASSES

- 1 cup (250ml) whole milk, chilled
- 4 tablespoons plain Greek yogurt
- 2 dessertspoons maple syrup
- 2 double shots espresso, cooled
- ice
- ½ teaspoon ground cardamom, plus extra for decorating

Blitz all the ingredients in a blender until well mixed. Serve over ice and decorate with a sprinkle of cardamom powder.

Nutty Banana and Coffee Milkshake
A delicious breakfast milkshake to start the day right.

MAKES 1 TALL GLASS
OR 2 SMALL GLASSES

- 2 shots espresso, cooled
- 1 small banana, chopped
- 1 teaspoon vanilla extract
- 1 teaspoon clear honey
- ⅔ cup (150ml) oat milk
- 1 rounded dessertspoon peanut butter
- whipped cream and grated chocolate, to serve

Blitz all the ingredients in a blender until smooth and creamy. Serve over ice and top with whipped cream and grated chocolate.

Coffee and Date Smoothie
The perfect way to kick-start your day.

MAKES 1 TALL GLASS

- 1 small banana
- 2 pitted dates
- 1 dessertspoon
  rolled oats
- 1 rounded dessertspoon
  tahini
- 1 tablespoon
  plain yogurt
- ½ teaspoon vanilla extract
- 2 shots espresso, cooled
- ⅔ cup (150ml) oat milk
- ice

Blitz all the ingredients in a blender until smooth. Serve over ice.

Mudslide
A rich, chocolaty, boozy milkshake, excellent as an after-dinner treat.

MAKES 1 GLASS

- 1½ tablespoons semi-sweet chocolate, melted
- 1 measure coffee liqueur
- 1 measure vodka
- 1 measure coffee cream liqueur
- 3½ tablespoons heavy cream
- ice

Place the melted chocolate in a saucer. Dip the rim of an old fashioned glass in to the melted chocolate, then allow the chocolate to drip down the glass. Place in the refrigerator for 10 minutes until hard. Add all the ingredients to a cocktail shaker with ice and shake well. Add some ice to the prepared glass, then strain the cocktail into it.

Wake the Dead
This cocktail is not for the faint hearted, but it will keep the party going! To make more than one drink, double or triple the ingredients accordingly.

MAKES 1

- ½ shot espresso, cooled
- 1 measure tequila
- 1 measure tequila-based coffee liqueur

Place all the ingredients in a cocktail shaker with ice and shake to mix. Strain into an old fashioned glass and serve ice cold.

How to Make Cold-Brew Coffee

Place ⅓ cup (50g) of ground coffee (your choice) into a large pitcher and add 1¾ cups (400ml) of cold water. Do not stir, just cover and allow to steep for 12–24 hours. Gently stir, then pour through a funnel lined with a paper coffee filter into another pitcher or large jar. Store in the refrigerator for up to two weeks.

Brew time: 12-24 hours

Brewing process: Brewed with cold or room-temperature water, never heated

Served: Diluted with water or milk, usually over ice

Flavor: Smooth, malty, or chocolaty rather than bitter and acidic

Storage: 10-14 days in the refrigerator

How to Make Iced Coffee

Simply make a hot pot of coffee, sweeten to taste with sugar (optional), and leave it to cool completely. Serve either black over ice or with your milk of choice.

Brew time: 20-30 minutes

Brewing process: Brewed hot, then cooled over ice

Served: Diluted with milk, often with sugar or flavored syrups, over ice

Flavor: Weaker than cold brew, due to melting ice, but more bitter

Storage: Drink within 24 hours

Espresso Tonic An easy-to-make, bubbly, and refreshing alternative to iced coffee.

MAKES 1 GLASS

- 1 shot espresso, cooled
- ice
- tonic water, chilled
- lime wedge, to serve

Brew a shot of espresso and let it cool. Add some ice to a glass and pour tonic water over the top, then pour in the espresso. Wipe the lime wedge around the rim of the glass, squeeze the juice into the drink, and then drop the wedge in.

Variations
- Use lemonade instead of tonic.
- Add a square of semi-sweet chocolate to the hot espresso, stir until melted, then cool.

Virgin Cold-Brew Colada

A delicious, cooling virgin colada with a coffee twist.

MAKES 2 TALL GLASSES

- ½ cup (120ml) cold-brew coffee (see page 46)
- 3½ tablespoons coconut cream
- 3½ tablespoons coconut plant-based milk
- 1½ tablespoons coconut syrup
- pineapple juice, to taste
- 1 slice of fresh pineapple, chopped, plus extra to decorate
- crushed ice, to serve

Blitz all the ingredients in a blender until smooth and creamy. Serve in a tall glass over crushed ice. Decorate the rim of the glass with a slice of pineapple.

Cold-Brew Soda
Sometimes hot milky coffee just doesn't cut it. This soda is cool, sweet, and refreshing.

MAKES 1 GLASS

- 2 tablespoons sugar syrup (see page 60)
- 2 shots cold-brew coffee (see page 46)
- ice
- soda water

Add sugar syrup to the cold-brew coffee and stir. Put some ice in a glass and add some soda water, but make sure you leave enough room to pour the coffee mixture over the top.

Minty Lemon Cold-Brew Soda

Muddle some mint leaves at the bottom of the glass, then add the juice of half a lemon and follow the instructions for Cold-Brew Soda.

Italian Sweet Coffee Cream

Add a spoonful to your coffee for an indulgent burst of sweet vanilla flavor—just like in Italy.

– 2½ cups (600ml)
whole milk
– 1 x 14 ounce (397g) can
of condensed milk
– 1 teaspoon vanilla extract

Gently heat the whole and condensed milk in a small saucepan to combine. Bring to a simmer while stirring, then remove from the heat. Allow the mixture to cool, then add the vanilla and stir. Pour into a sterilized jar or container and store for up to 10 days in the refrigerator.

Coffee and Banana Smoothie Bowl

This energizing bowl of sweet and creamy goodness with a coffee kick is the best way to start your day.

SERVES 1

- 1 medium frozen banana
- 1 shot espresso, cooled
- ½ cup (120ml) oat milk
- 1 rounded dessertspoon almond or peanut butter
- 1 level dessertspoon chocolate protein powder
- 2 level dessertspoons rolled oats

Toppings:
- blueberries
- desiccated coconut or coconut chips
- maple syrup, to drizzle

Blitz all the main ingredients in a blender until smooth. Pour into a bowl and decorate with toppings.

Mocha and Amaretto Mousse

A delicious and simple dessert, perfect for any coffee and chocolate lover.

SERVES 4

- ½ cup (75g) semi-sweet chocolate, chopped
- 1 shot espresso
- 1 measure amaretto liqueur
- 3 medium eggs
- 3 teaspoons sugar

To serve:
- whipped cream
- grated chocolate
- soft amaretti cookies, crumbled

Melt the chocolate over a bain-marie or in a microwave on low, slowly. Add the espresso and liqueur and stir well. Separate the yolks and egg whites into separate bowls. Whisk the egg whites with the sugar until they form peaks. Whisk the melted chocolate into the egg yolks then gently fold in the egg whites until the mixture is a uniform chocolate color. Pour into four small glass dishes and chill in the refrigerator for at least 1 hour. Serve decorated with whipped cream, grated chocolate, and crumbled cookies.

Creamy Coffee Panna Cotta

This silky dessert is the perfect way to end dinner—cooling and not too filling.

SERVES 4

- 1 cup (250ml) whole milk
- 1 level tablespoon powdered gelatin
- 3 tablespoons superfine sugar
- 2 teaspoons instant espresso powder
- 1 cup (250ml) heavy cream
- Coffee Syrup (see page 61), to serve

Add the milk to a small saucepan, sprinkle the gelatin over the top, and leave for 5 minutes until it is wrinkled. Gently warm the milk to dissolve the gelatin, but do not boil. Add the sugar and espresso powder and simmer. Stir well, then take off the heat. Add the cream to the pan and stir well again. Pour into four martini glasses, then leave to set and cool in the refrigerator for about 3 hours. Serve with a drizzle of Coffee Syrup on top.

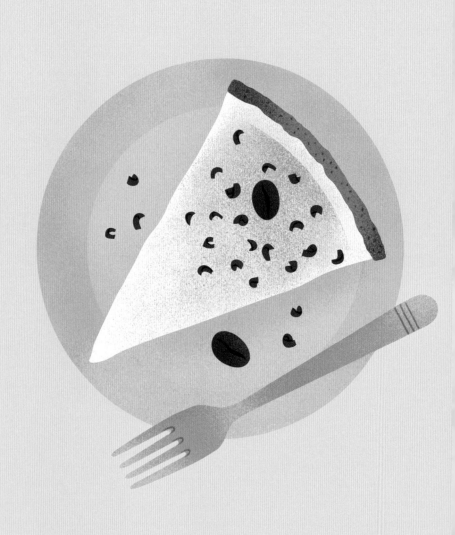

No-Bake Creamy Coffee Cheesecake

This cheesecake is simple to make and has a light and creamy coffee flavor. It is delicious, impressive, and guaranteed to be a dinner-party hit.

SERVES 8

For the base:
- 1¾ cups (200g) graham crackers
- ¼ cup (50g) salted butter, melted
- 2 tablespoons strong-brewed coffee

For the filling:
- 1¾ cups (400g) cream cheese
- ¾ cup + 2 tablespoons (100g) confectioners' sugar
- 2 shots espresso, cooled
- 1½ cups (350g) heavy cream
- 4 tablespoons milk
- 3 teaspoons gelatin powder

You will also need:
- 8-9 inch (20-23cm) springform pan
- grated chocolate, to serve

To make the base, crush the graham crackers into crumbs, add the melted butter and coffee, and mix well. Press the mixture into the bottom of a springform pan. Put the pan in the refrigerator to chill while you make the filling.

To make the filling, beat together the cream cheese, sugar, and espresso until creamy and smooth. In a separate large bowl, beat the cream until it thickens and forms stiff peaks. Add the milk to a small pan and sprinkle the gelatin over the top. Leave for about 5 minutes until it is wrinkled, then gently warm the milk to dissolve the gelatin. Stir well. Add some of the cream cheese mixture to the gelatin and stir well again, then fold the gelatin mixture into the rest of the cream cheese, add the cream, and stir well. Spoon the filling onto the cheesecake base and smooth out using a palette knife. Cover and refrigerate for 4-5 hours. The cheesecake must be firm before you attempt to remove it from the pan. Run a knife around the edge before releasing it from the pan. Serve sprinkled with grated chocolate.

Tiramisu Pots

These individual desserts are easier to make than the classic version and are equally delicious.

SERVES 4

- 1 egg yolk
- 2 dessertspoons superfine sugar
- 1 teaspoon vanilla extract
- ¾ cup (200ml) heavy cream
- 2 tablespoons mascarpone
- 12 ladyfingers
- grated semi-sweet chocolate, to serve

For the syrup:
- ¾ cup (200ml) espresso, cooled
- 2 tablespoons dark coffee liqueur

To make the sweet cream, whisk together the egg yolk, sugar, and vanilla in a bowl. Add the cream and mascarpone and whisk well until creamy and forming peaks.

To make the coffee syrup, add the espresso and liqueur to a bowl and stir.

Make one dessert at a time. Allow three ladyfingers per dessert. Break each ladyfinger into three pieces and dip into the coffee mixture, then place the three pieces at the bottom of a small glass and put a large dessertspoonful of the cream on top. Repeat twice more to create three layers of cream and sponge. Finish each dessert with a drizzle of the coffee mixture and some grated chocolate. Once you have made all the desserts, transfer them to the refrigerator until just before serving.

Flavored Syrups These syrups are a good way to add different flavors to drinks and desserts.

Simple Sugar Syrup

This can be used to sweeten cocktails or coffees. It's a good basic recipe that is easy to add flavors to. Simply add 3½ cups (700g) of superfine sugar to a small saucepan, then add ⅓ cup (100ml) of cold water and heat gently to dissolve the sugar. Cool and pour into a sterilized jar or bottle. Store in the refrigerator for up to a month. Makes ⅓ cup (100ml) of syrup.

Vanilla: Add 1 teaspoon of vanilla extract with the scrapings of 1 vanilla bean pod to cooled Simple Sugar Syrup. Sieve before using.

Cinnamon: Add two cinnamon sticks to cooled Simple Sugar Syrup and allow to steep for 6 hours. Sieve before using.

Ginger: Add 1 inch (2.5cm) of peeled and sliced ginger to cooled Simple Sugar Syrup and allow to steep for a couple of hours. Sieve before using.

Coffee Syrup
This thin syrup is easy to make and delicious in milkshakes and cocktails.

SERVES 4

- 1¼ cups (250g) brown sugar
- 1 cup (250ml) strong-brewed coffee
- 1 teaspoon vanilla extract

Add the sugar and coffee to a saucepan and stir over a gentle heat until all the sugar has dissolved. Remove from the heat and stir in the vanilla. Cool completely and strain into a sterilized container. Store in the refrigerator for up to four weeks.

Sweet

Here are sweet treats galore, made even more delicious with plenty of coffee to flavor them—truffles to give as presents or secretly steal from the refrigerator, cakes that can be made in minutes when you need a sugar hit, and impressive desserts that are easy to make.

Mocha Truffles
Chocolaty with a hint of coffee. Serve with a pot of fresh coffee for maximum pleasure.

MAKES ABOUT 20

- ⅔ cup (150ml) heavy cream
- 1⅔ cups (250g) mix of semi-sweet and milk chocolate, finely chopped
- 1½ tablespoons butter, cubed
- 1 tablespoon instant espresso powder
- boiling water
- 1 tablespoon dark coffee liqueur
- confectioners' sugar or cocoa powder, to coat

Heat the cream to boiling point in a small pan. Remove from the heat, add the chocolate and butter, and stir until melted and well mixed. Make the espresso powder into a paste with boiling water. Transfer the chocolate mixture to a bowl, add the espresso paste and liqueur, and stir until smooth. Then cool in the refrigerator for a couple of hours or overnight, until the mixture is firm.

Add some confectioners' sugar or cocoa powder to a wide bowl. Use a teaspoon to scoop out walnut-size amounts of the mixture, roll into balls, and cover in the confectioners' sugar or cocoa powder. It is important to have cool hands and to work quickly. Once you have made all the truffles, store them in the refrigerator until serving, as they will soften at room temperature. They can be kept in the refrigerator for up to a week.

Coffee Creams
Another winning coffee and chocolate combination. These delicious treats will melt in your mouth.

- 1 egg white
- 2¾ cups (350g) confectioners' sugar, sifted
- 2 heaped teaspoons instant espresso powder
- 3½ tablespoons semi-sweet chocolate, melted, for drizzling or dipping

You will also need:
- cookie sheet
- parchment paper

Whisk the egg white until it is bubbly and frothy. Gently mix the sugar and coffee powder together with a fork. Add the egg white to the sugar mixture, a little at a time, to make a firm dough. Knead well, using your hands. Place the dough on a chopping board that has been dusted with confectioners' sugar and roll it out until it is about ¼ inch (5mm) thick. Using a small, coin-sized cutter, cut out 30 candies. Transfer the candies onto a cookie sheet lined with parchment paper and leave them to harden overnight in the refrigerator. Once hard, use a fork or teaspoon to drizzle melted chocolate back and forth over the candies, then return them to the refrigerator to set for an hour before serving.

Golden Toffee Popcorn
Fill cellophane bags with this popcorn and tie with ribbon for a great gift.

MAKES 1
MEDIUM BOWL

- 4 cups (125g) Plain Popcorn (see below)
- 2 shots espresso
- ⅔ cup (125g) superfine sugar
- 4 tablespoons dark corn syrup
- ½ tablespoon butter
- ½ teaspoon instant espresso powder

Place the popcorn in a large mixing bowl. Add the espresso, sugar, syrup, and butter to a saucepan and gently heat. Stir until the butter has melted and everything is well mixed. Add the espresso powder and stir again. Drizzle the coffee mixture over the popcorn and stir. Allow the popcorn to cool, then break it up and store in an airtight container.

Plain Popcorn

Add 4 tablespoons of vegetable oil to a large saucepan over medium heat. Add 1 cup (125g) of popcorn kernels to the pan and swirl to coat in the oil. Wait for the kernels to start popping, gently shaking the pan occasionally. Once the popping has stopped, remove the pan from the heat and allow the popcorn to cool.

Maple and Coffee Nuts A delicious
sweet snack to serve after dinner, with coffee.

MAKES 3 ⅓ CUPS
(500G)

- 4 tablespoons
  brown sugar
- 2 tablespoons maple syrup
- 3 teaspoons instant
  espresso powder
- 1 teaspoon ground
  Himalayan salt
- 3 tablespoons cold water
- 3⅓ cups (500g) roasted
  unsalted mixed nuts
- 1 teaspoon vanilla extract

You will also need:
- cookie sheet
- parchment paper

Preheat the oven to 350°F. Place the sugar, syrup, espresso powder, and salt in a small saucepan. Add the water and gently heat until simmering and well mixed. Simmer until all the sugar has dissolved, then take off the heat and add the nuts and vanilla. Stir well to coat the nuts, then transfer them to a cookie sheet lined with parchment paper. Spread the syrup-coated nuts out and bake in the oven for approximately 15 minutes—the coating on the nuts should feel slightly tacky. Set aside to cool for 30–40 minutes, then break up and serve.

Cardamom and Coffee Mug Cake

An easy cake that can be made in minutes, perfect for when you fancy something sweet.

MAKES 1 MUG CAKE

- butter, for greasing
- 2 tablespoons
  self-rising flour
- 2 dessertspoons
  brown sugar
- 1 medium egg
- 2 teaspoons olive oil
- ½ teaspoon vanilla extract
- ½ teaspoon cardamom
  powder
- 1 level teaspoon instant
  espresso powder

Butter the inside of a large mug. Add all the ingredients to the mug and mix well with a fork—try to get rid of as many lumps as possible. Microwave on high for 1 minute, or until risen and sponge-like. Let cool for 1 minute, then tuck in. Best eaten warm.

Cinnamon and Coffee Toast This recipe
makes an easy weekend breakfast or late-night snack.

MAKES 4 SLICES

- 2 eggs, beaten
- 3½ tablespoons
  whole milk
- 1 shot espresso, cooled
- 1 tablespoon maple syrup
- 1 teaspoon vanilla extract
- ½ teaspoon ground
  cinnamon
- 4 medium slices
  white bread
- butter, for frying
- maple syrup and crispy
  bacon, to serve

Whisk the eggs, milk, espresso, maple syrup,
vanilla, and cinnamon together in a wide bowl
to make a smooth batter. Soak the bread in the
batter, a slice at a time. Heat a heavy-based
skillet to medium heat, then add butter to the
pan—a couple of teaspoons for each slice.
Melt the butter and fry each slice for about 2-3
minutes on each side, until golden brown and
crisp. Cut the toast in half and serve drizzled
with maple syrup and crispy bacon.

Chocolate and Coffee Fridge Cake

Fridge cakes are easy to make, and this one is perfect for a late-afternoon sugar and caffeine hit!

MAKES 16 SQUARES

- 1 cup + 2 tablespoons (200g) milk chocolate, chopped
- ½ cup (100g) butter
- ⅔ cup (150ml) dark corn syrup
- 1 dessertspoon instant espresso powder
- 2 cups (200g) graham crackers, crushed
- confectioners' sugar, for dusting

You will also need:
- 8 inch (20cm) square brownie pan
- heat-safe plastic wrap

Line a brownie pan with plastic wrap. Gently melt the chocolate, butter, and syrup in a saucepan over low heat. Add the espresso powder and stir well, then add the crushed graham crackers and stir again. Spoon the mixture into the brownie pan and smooth out. Chill in the refrigerator for a couple of hours, or until hardened. Cut into 16 squares, dust with confectioners' sugar, and serve with a cup of coffee.

Roasted Pears A simple but impressive
dessert to serve at a dinner party.

SERVES 4

– 4 large, ripe pears
– superfine sugar,
  for sprinkling
– 1½ tablespoons
  butter, melted,
  for drizzling
– Glossy Coffee Sauce
  (see below) and vanilla
  ice cream, to serve

Preheat the oven to 350°F. Peel, core, and halve
your pears and place them face down in a lightly
oiled roasting pan. Lightly sprinkle with the
sugar then drizzle with the butter. Cook in the
oven for approximately 40 minutes, or until soft
and golden. Drizzle with Glossy Coffee Sauce
and serve with vanilla ice cream.

Glossy Coffee Sauce Perfect over roasted
pears and vanilla ice cream.

– ¾ cup + 2 tablespoons
  (175g) superfine sugar
– 1½ tablespoons butter
– 3 shots espresso
– ¾ cup (175ml) water
– 3½ tablespoons
  whipping cream
– 1 small pinch of salt

Gently heat the sugar and butter in a saucepan
with the espresso and water until it all melts.
Stir well, then bring to a boil. Reduce the heat
and simmer until the sauce reduces to become
thick and glossy. Remove from the heat and
whisk in the cream and a pinch of salt. The
sauce should look glossy and have a sticky
texture. If it is too runny, return to the heat and
boil for a couple more minutes. Serve with
Roasted Pears (see above).

Japanese Coffee Jelly An elegant dessert
that looks as good as it tastes.

SERVES 4

– 3 teaspoons
  gelatin powder
– 4 shots espresso
– ⅓ cup (75g) brown sugar
– ¾ cup (180ml)
  boiling water
– 1 cup (240ml) cold water
– heavy cream, to serve

Put the gelatin, espresso, and sugar into a large
pitcher and pour the boiling water over the
ingredients. Whisk well until the gelatin and sugar
have dissolved. Add the cold water and whisk
well again. Pour the jelly into martini glasses
and place in the refrigerator for approximately 3
hours, or until set. Serve with heavy cream poured
on top to make a creamy layer.

Mocha Tart
A deliciously rich tart, perfect for special occasions.

SERVES 8

- 1 sheet of pie dough, chilled
- 1¼ cups (300ml) heavy cream
- 1 tablespoon superfine sugar
- 1 tablespoon instant espresso powder
- 1 cup + 2 tablespoons (200g) semi-sweet chocolate, chopped
- ¼ cup (50g) salted butter
- cream or ice cream, to serve

You will also need:
- 7 inch (18cm) round tart pan
- heat-safe plastic wrap
- ceramic baking beans

Preheat the oven to 375°F. Roll out the pie dough. Line the tin with the pastry, then trim off any excess. Top the pie dough with heat-safe plastic wrap and add ceramic baking beans. Cook the pie dough for 20 minutes, remove the beans and plastic wrap, and cook for a further 5 minutes. Set the pie crust aside to cool.

Gently warm the cream, sugar, espresso powder, chocolate, and butter over low heat until melted and stir well. Take the mixture off the heat. Stir, then leave to cool for 10 minutes before pouring into the pie crust. Do not fill the pie crust to the top. Cool the tart in the refrigerator for a couple of hours, or until set, before serving. Serve with cream or ice cream.

Espresso Risotto with Roasted Oranges Coffee and orange flavors give this dish an unexpected twist.

SERVES 4

- 2 cups (450ml) whole milk
- 2 tablespoons sugar
- ½ cup (100g) risotto rice
- 2 tablespoons dark coffee liqueur
- 2 shots espresso
- roasted oranges, to serve

For the roasted oranges:
- 2 oranges
- olive oil
- sugar
- ground cinnamon

You will also need:
- cookie sheet
- aluminum foil

Warm the milk and sugar in a large saucepan on the stovetop. Once simmering, add the rice and stir. Cook the risotto gently for 20-25 minutes, or until the rice has softened but retains bite.
Add a little more milk if the rice becomes too dry. Stir in the liqueur and coffee and mix well. Gently cook for another 5-10 minutes or until you have your desired consistency. Serve in coffee cups with roasted oranges on the side.

Roasted oranges
Preheat the oven to 350°C. Line a cookie sheet with aluminum foil. Slice two oranges into rounds. Place the rounds on the cookie sheet, drizzle with a little olive oil, and sprinkle with a little sugar and ground cinnamon. Bake in the oven for about 15-20 minutes. Serve with the Espresso Risotto, allowing approximately half an orange per person.

WHAT TO DO WITH LEFTOVER COFFEE GROUNDS

If you're regularly making coffee at home, you're going to find yourself with a lot of leftover grounds. Rather than just throwing them away, try these ideas.

FERTILIZE YOUR GARDEN

Coffee grounds contain nitrogen, calcium, potassium, iron, phosphorus, magnesium, and chromium, all of which will help fertilize your soil, nourish your plants, and attract worms. Simply sprinkle cooled leftover grounds onto your soil.

ADD TO COMPOST

Compost made with plant food waste and coffee grounds is nutrient rich and very good for the garden. Adding coffee grounds to compost also helps to decrease greenhouse gas emissions.

MAKE A BODY OR LIP SCRUB

Coarse coffee grounds are good for exfoliation. Melt a small amount of coconut oil in a bowl in the microwave. Add a couple of spoonfuls of grounds and mix well. Rub into your hands and body to help remove dead skin cells, then rinse off in the shower. To make a lip scrub, add honey to some grounds and use on your lips.

MAKE A NATURAL DYE

If you are making a costume and want to age an old white T-shirt, simply add a little water to some coffee grounds to create a natural dye that works on paper, cotton, and linen.

TENDERIZE MEAT

The acidity in coffee helps to keep meat soft and tender, and also enhances flavor. Add coffee grounds to your steak with salt and oil for tasty flavor and a crisp crust.

TREAT SCRATCHES ON FURNITURE

Before purchasing a commercial treatment, try using some coffee grounds on your scratched furniture. Make a thick paste by adding water to the grounds. Rub the mixture into the scratch and leave it for 5-10 minutes, then remove with a clean cloth. Repeat this process until you get the required color match—you might have to leave the coffee on for longer if you need to achieve a strong color.

Baked

The joys of baking are well known—the relaxing stirring, the delicious aromas that pervade the kitchen, and that first taste of a warm cookie, fresh from the oven. There is nothing not to like about making cakes, cookies, and bread, and these bakes made with coffee are perfect for breakfast, lunch, and dinner.

Chocolate and Coffee Cookies Golden, crisp, and chewy, and perfect to serve with coffee.

MAKES 16 COOKIES

- ½ cup + 1 tablespoon (125g) salted butter
- ⅔ cup (125g) superfine sugar
- ½ teaspoon baking powder
- 1 cup + 2 tablespoons (150g) all-purpose flour
- 1 large egg, beaten
- 1 level tablespoon instant espresso powder, mixed with a little water to make a paste
- ¾ cup (150g) milk or semi-sweet chocolate, finely chopped

You will also need:
- cookie sheet
- parchment paper

Preheat the oven to 350°F. Cream the butter and sugar together until light and fluffy. Add baking powder to the flour and gently mix. Add a little of the egg to the butter mixture, alternating with a little of the flour, stirring in between each addition, until all used up. Add the espresso paste and stir, then add the chocolate and gently fold in.

Line a cookie sheet with parchment paper. Spoon 8 dessertspoons of the mixture onto the tray, leaving room in between each spoonful as the cookies will spread. Bake in the preheated oven for about 12 minutes, or until golden, crispy around the edge, and soft in the middle. Remove the cookies to cool and bake the second batch.

Coffee Kisses
These cookies, sandwiched together with Coffee Buttercream, are an excellent addition to a morning or afternoon cup of coffee.

MAKES 12

- 2½ teaspoons instant espresso powder
- 1 teaspoon boiling water
- 1 cup + 2 tablespoons (150g) self-rising flour
- ⅓ cup + 1 tablespoon (75g) superfine sugar
- ⅓ cup (75g) unsalted butter, cubed
- 1 medium egg, beaten
- Coffee Buttercream (see page 85), for sandwiching

You will also need:
- cookie sheet
- parchment paper

Preheat the oven to 350°F. Add the espresso powder to a cup, then add the boiling water, mix to a paste, and set aside to cool. Add the flour and sugar to a large mixing bowl and gently mix. Add the butter to the flour mixture and rub in using your fingertips until you have a coarse crumb-like texture. Add the beaten egg to the cooled coffee and gently beat using a fork. Add the coffee mixture to the crumb mixture and work in using a fork, then use your hands to make a soft dough. Knead the dough well.

Line a large cookie sheet with parchment paper, then, using your hands, roll the dough into 24 walnut-size balls. Place half of them onto the cookie sheet and flatten, leaving space between each for spreading. You will need to make two batches of 12 cookies. Bake each batch in the oven for about 15 minutes, or until golden. Allow the cookies to cool, then sandwich them together with the Coffee Buttercream to make perfect kisses.

Coffee Buttercream

This recipe makes enough buttercream to sandwich together a cake and ice the top, or to sandwich together a full batch of Coffee Kisses (see page 84).

- 1 rounded teaspoon instant espresso powder
- 1 teaspoon boiling water
- ½ cup (100g) unsalted butter, softened
- 1⅔ cups (200g) confectioners' sugar, sifted

Add the espresso powder to a cup, then add the boiling water, mix to a paste, and set aside to cool. Beat the butter and sugar together until soft and fluffy. Add the cooled coffee mixture and beat well together.

Simple Biscotti

These easy-to-make Italian treats originated in Tuscany in the 14th century. The word *biscotti* means "twice baked." While biscotti don't contain coffee, they are the perfect shape and crunchiness for serving with and dipping in coffee.

MAKES 25

- 1 cup (150g) shelled almonds
- 2 medium eggs
- ¾ cup (150g) superfine sugar
- zest of 1 lemon
- 2⅓ cups (300g) all-purpose flour
- 1 teaspoon baking powder

You will also need:
- cookie sheet
- parchment paper

Preheat the oven to 400°F. Roast the almonds on a cookie sheet for about 5 minutes and then chop them roughly. Beat the eggs and the sugar together well, until pale in color and increased in size. Add the nuts and the zest, then sift in the flour and baking powder. Mix well, then use your hands to form a dough. Divide the dough into two, then roll each half out on a floured countertop using your hands, to make two long log shapes about 1½ inches (4cm) wide and 10 inches (25cm) long.

Place the logs on a lined cookie sheet and bake for 20 minutes, or until just golden. Reduce the oven to 300°F. Let the logs cool for a few minutes, then slice them into long pieces about ½ inch (1cm) wide using a sharp bread knife. Lay them back on the cookie sheet and return to the oven for another 15–20 minutes, to dry out. They should be crispy, crunchy, and golden. Serve them with coffee, always.

Honey-Drizzled Espresso Cakes

These cupcakes are sticky, sweet, and delicious
with a light coffee and honey flavor.

MAKES 12

- ⅔ cup (150g) salted
  butter, softened
- ¾ cup (150g)
  muscovado sugar
- 1¼ cups (175g)
  self-rising flour
- 3 large eggs, beaten
- boiling water
- 3 teaspoons instant
  espresso powder

For the honey drizzle:
- 4 teaspoons honey
- ½ cup (50g) confectioners'
  sugar, sifted
- 1–2 teaspoons water

You will also need:
- 12-hole muffin pan
- paper baking cups

Preheat the oven to 350°F and line a muffin pan
with baking cups. Cream the butter and sugar in
a mixing bowl until light and fluffy. Add the flour
and eggs alternately, a little of each at a time,
stirring well. Add a splash of boiling water to the
coffee powder and mix, then add the coffee to the
cake batter and stir in well. Add a dessertspoon
of the cake batter to each of the baking cups and
bake for 20 minutes in the preheated oven. Allow
the cakes to cool.

To make the drizzle, add the honey to the
confectioners' sugar and add the water a
teaspoon at a time, mixing well until thick but
runny. Drizzle back and forth over the top of the
cooled cakes using a teaspoon. Let the drizzle set
before serving. Alternatively, top the cakes with
Coffee Buttercream (see page 85), if preferred.

Marbled Mocha Loaf with
Vanilla Glaze
A blend of coffee, chocolate, and vanilla gives this cake an unbeatable flavor and an impressive appearance.

– ½ cup + 1 tablespoon
  (125g) salted butter
– ⅔ cup (125g)
  superfine sugar
– 1 teaspoon baking powder
– 1 cup (125g)
  self-rising flour
– 2 eggs, beaten
– 1 teaspoon vanilla extract
– 1 teaspoon instant
  espresso powder
– 1 teaspoon cocoa powder
– boiling water
– butter, for greasing
– Vanilla Glaze (see page 91)

You will also need:
– loaf pan
– parchment paper

Preheat the oven to 350°F. Cream the butter and sugar together until light and fluffy. Add the baking powder to the flour and stir. Add a little of the egg and stir, then add a little sifted flour and mix. Repeat, alternating, until all the egg and flour are used up. Stir the batter well, then divide evenly into two separate bowls.

Add the vanilla to one bowl and stir. Mix the espresso powder and cocoa powder together and add a splash of boiling water to make a smooth paste. Add the paste to the other bowl and stir. Grease and line a loaf pan with parchment paper. To get a marbled effect, spoon the two batters into the pan to create a checkered pattern. Build up layers by placing the mocha batter on top of the vanilla and vice versa. Gently run a fork through the batters to create a marbled pattern.

Bake in the preheated oven for about 45 minutes, or until the top is springy to touch and an inserted knife or toothpick comes out clean. Transfer the cake to a wire rack to cool. Once cooled, drizzle the top of the cake with Vanilla Glaze. Let the glaze set before serving.

Vanilla Glaze
This glaze works well on biscuits and doughnuts as well as cakes. Drizzle it back and forth using a teaspoon or fork.

- 1¼ cups (150g) confectioners' sugar
- 3 tablespoons low-fat milk, plus extra if needed
- 2 teaspoons vanilla extract

Sift the confectioners' sugar into a bowl and add the milk and vanilla, a little at a time. Stir well until you have a pourable glaze. If the mixture is too stiff, add extra milk a teaspoon at a time until you achieve the right consistency.

Mocha Brownies with Salted Caramel Sauce Rich and fudgy, with a smooth and salty topping.

MAKES 16

- 1 cup + 2 tablespoons (200g) semi-sweet chocolate, chopped
- ¾ cup (175g) butter
- 2 tablespoons instant espresso powder
- 3 medium eggs
- 1 cup (200g) superfine sugar
- 1 teaspoon vanilla extract
- 1 tablespoon maple syrup
- ¾ cup (100g) self-rising flour
- 1 cup + 2 tablespoons (200g) milk chocolate, chopped
- Salted Caramel Sauce (see page 93), to serve

You will also need:
- 9 inch (23cm) square brownie pan
- parchment paper

Preheat the oven to 350°F. Grease and line a brownie pan with parchment paper. Melt the semi-sweet chocolate and butter in a heat-safe bowl in the microwave, 10 seconds at a time, then stir to mix in the coffee. In a separate bowl, beat the eggs and sugar together, then add the chocolate mixture, vanilla, and maple syrup. Sift in the flour and stir until thick and glossy. Fold the chopped milk chocolate into the mixture and pour into the lined pan. Use a spatula to spread the mixture out, then bake in the oven for approximately 30 minutes, or until crispy on the outside and soft and fudgy in the middle. Plunge the bottom of the pan into cold water to stop the cooking, taking care not to get the brownies wet, then cool fully in the tin. Cut into 16 squares and serve with Salted Caramel Sauce.

Salted Caramel Sauce

Delicious on all desserts and ice cream, but especially good on brownies. Also perfect eaten cold for a late-night snack!

MAKES ENOUGH FOR
16 BROWNIES

- ¾ cup + 2 tablespoons (175g) brown sugar
- 1¼ cups (300ml) heavy cream
- ¼ cup (50g) salted butter
- ½ teaspoon salt

Add all the ingredients to a small saucepan and gently warm on the stovetop, stirring continuously until the sugar has dissolved. Turn up the heat so that the sauce bubbles and becomes golden and glossy. Stir well, then remove from the heat and allow to cool before serving. Serve with Mocha Brownies (see page 92).

Coffee and Date Sheet Cake

This sweet treat is rich and full of flavor. Using pre-made pie dough makes it quick and easy to prepare, ready to enjoy with a mid-morning or after-dinner coffee.

MAKES 16 SLICES

- 1 cup + 2 tablespoons (250g) pitted dates, chopped
- ⅓ cup (75ml) espresso
- zest of half an orange
- 2 sheets pie dough
- butter, for greasing
- milk, for glazing
- superfine sugar, for sprinkling

You will also need:
- 7 inch (20cm) square brownie pan
- parchment paper

Preheat the oven to 400°F. Place the dates, espresso, and orange zest in a saucepan on the stovetop and gently warm for about 4-5 minutes or until the mixture is soft and sticky. Set aside to cool. Butter a brownie pan and line with parchment paper. Cut one of the sheets of pie dough so that it fits the base and gently press it into the corners. Spread the cooled date mixture over the pie dough then top with the second pie dough sheet that has been cut to size. Gently push the pie dough down and into the corners. Bake in the oven for 25-30 minutes, or until golden brown. Allow to cool in the pan then cut into approximately 16 slices.

MATCHING FLAVORS WITH COFFEE

Coffee obviously goes well with milk, sugar, and chocolate, but there are so many other flavors that make a perfect pairing with coffee, either as an addition to a drink or to complement a cup of coffee. Coffee has many notes that make it a great match for a range of different flavors:

- Almond
- Banana
- Beef
- Berries
- Black currant
- Caramel
- Cardamom
- Chai
- Cheese
- Chocolate
- Cinnamon
- Coconut
- Ginger
- Hazelnut
- Mint
- Nutmeg
- Orange
- Pumpkin
- Rose
- Vanilla
- Walnut

Cappuccino Cake with Creamy Frosting
A modern update on traditional coffee cake. All walnuts have been banished, replaced by creamy frosting topped with grated chocolate.

SERVES 8-10

- 1½ cups (200g) self-rising flour
- 1 teaspoon baking powder
- 2 teaspoons instant espresso powder
- ¾ cup + 2 tablespoons (200g) unsalted butter, softened
- ½ cup (100g) superfine sugar
- ½ cup (100g) light brown sugar
- 4 medium eggs, beaten
- boiling water
- Creamy Vanilla Frosting (see below), for sandwiching and topping
- grated milk chocolate, to decorate

You will also need:
- 2 x 9 inch (23cm) springform pans

Preheat the oven to 350°F. Gently mix the flour, baking powder, and espresso powder together. Beat the butter with the sugars until soft, light, and fluffy. Add a little of the egg and stir, then a little sifted flour and mix. Repeat, alternating, until all the egg and flour are used up. For a smooth and glossy cake batter, add a splash of boiling water and stir well. Divide the batter between two well-greased springform pans. Bake in the oven for approximately 20 minutes or until golden and an inserted knife or toothpick comes out clean. Remove the cakes from the pans and allow them to cool. Sandwich the cakes together with the frosting and spread the remaining frosting onto the top of the cake using a palette knife. Top with grated chocolate.

Creamy Vanilla Frosting

Place 2 cups (250g) of sifted confectioners' sugar, ⅓ cup (80g) of softened unsalted butter, 2 tablespoons of whole milk, and a ½ teaspoon of vanilla extract in a bowl and beat until light, fluffy, and creamy. This will be enough to sandwich a cake together and cover the top.

Coffee and Banana Cake

This alternative to classic banana bread is boosted by coffee and golden raisins. It's an excellent way to use up any ripe bananas in the fruit bowl.

SERVES 8-10

- ½ cup (75g) golden raisins
- 2 measures dark coffee liqueur
- 1¼ cups (175g) self-rising flour
- 2 teaspoons instant espresso powder
- ½ cup + 1 tablespoon (125g) salted butter, melted, plus extra for greasing
- ½ tablespoon superfine sugar
- 2 large eggs, beaten
- 3 medium ripe bananas, mashed

You will also need:
- small loaf pan
- parchment paper

Preheat the oven to 350°F. Place the golden raisins in a small bowl and pour the coffee liqueur over them, and leave them to steep while you prepare the cake batter. Place the flour and espresso powder in a large mixing bowl and stir to combine. In another large mixing bowl, mix the melted butter and sugar until blended, then add the beaten eggs and the mashed bananas and stir well together. Drain the golden raisins and add them to the butter mixture with a couple of teaspoons of the leftover liqueur. Add the flour a tablespoon at a time and mix well to get a lumpy, speckled batter. Grease a loaf pan and line it with parchment paper. Spoon the batter into the pan and bake for about 1 hour, or until golden and an inserted knife or toothpick comes out clean— the top of the cake should bounce back when pressed. Eat warm from the oven or set aside to cool and store in an airtight container.

Coffee Soda Bread
This lovely dense bread is best eaten warm with butter.

MAKES 1 LOAF

- 2⅓ cups (300g) all-purpose flour, plus extra for sprinkling
- 1 teaspoon baking powder
- 2 tablespoons instant espresso powder
- ⅓ cup + 1 tablespoon (75g) superfine sugar
- 1¼ cups (300ml) buttermilk

Preheat the oven to 350°F. Mix the flour, baking powder, espresso powder, and sugar in a bowl, then add the buttermilk. Using your hands, bring it all together into a dough. Turn the dough out onto a floured countertop, knead for about 1 minute, then shape into a ball. Flatten the ball a little then cut a deep cross into the top. Sprinkle the top with a little flour then bake in the oven for about 40 minutes, or until the bottom of the loaf sounds hollow when tapped.

Coffee Butter
Serve this delicious butter on toast, bread, or pancakes.

- ½ teaspoon boiled water
- 1 teaspoon instant espresso powder
- ¼ cup (50g) salted butter, softened
- 1 dessertspoon confectioners' sugar

Make a paste by adding the boiled water to the espresso powder. Beat the butter, sugar, and espresso paste together with a spoon until smooth. Serve immediately or store in the refrigerator.

Coffee Scones

Eat these warm from the oven with butter—or Coffee Butter for extra flavor.

MAKES 15

- 2⅓ cups (300g) all-purpose flour, sifted
- ⅔ cup (125g) superfine sugar
- 2 teaspoons baking powder
- ½ teaspoon salt
- ½ cup (100g) chilled salted butter, cubed
- ¼ cup (50ml) strong-brewed coffee
- 2 teaspoons instant espresso powder
- 1 teaspoon vanilla extract
- ½ cup (120ml) buttermilk
- 1 large egg, beaten
- butter or Coffee Butter (see page 100), to serve

You will also need:
- 2¼ inch (6cm) round cookie cutter
- cookie sheet
- parchment paper

Preheat the oven to 400°F. Gently mix the flour, sugar, baking powder, and salt in a large bowl. Add the butter to the flour mix and rub in using your fingertips until you have a fine, crumb-like texture. In a separate bowl, mix the coffee, espresso powder, and vanilla. Allow to cool, then add the buttermilk and the egg and mix well.

Make a well in your crumb mixture and add the coffee mixture, then gently stir until you have a crumbly dough. The dough will be quite sticky, so ensure you have a well-floured countertop to knead on—add extra flour if necessary. Gently knead the dough, then roll out on the floured countertop until the dough is about ½–¾ inch (1.5–2cm) thick. Using a cookie cutter, cut out your scones and chill in the refrigerator for 20 minutes on a lined cookie sheet; leave room between each scone as they will spread. Brush a little milk onto the top of the scones, then bake in the oven for 20 minutes, or until golden brown and cooked through. Serve with butter or Coffee Butter.

Iced

Unleash the blender, empty the freezer, and rejoice at these ice-laden drinks, popsicles, and desserts—perfect for summer parties, post-workout treats, or enjoying by the pool. Easy to make, iced to perfection, and just what you need on hot days.

Coconut Frappé Tropical and refreshing— a perfect summer drink.

SERVES 2

– 1¼ cups (300ml) plant-based coconut milk
– 2 tablespoons coconut syrup
– 1 dessertspoon instant espresso powder
– 4 ice cubes
– whipped cream, to serve
– grated chocolate, to serve

Blitz the coconut milk, coconut syrup, and espresso powder in a blender on low until mixed. Add the ice cubes one by one, and blitz again until frothy. Serve topped with whipped cream and grated chocolate.

Croatian Iced Coffee So much more
than just coffee on ice!

SERVES 2

- 2 shots espresso
- 2 dessertspoons Chocolate Syrup (see below)
- 2 scoops vanilla ice cream
- 1¼ cups (300ml) milk
- 4 ice cubes
- whipped cream, to serve
- grated chocolate, to serve

Blitz the espresso, syrup, ice cream, and milk in a blender on low until mixed. Add the ice cubes one by one, and blitz again. Serve topped with whipped cream and grated chocolate.

Chocolate Syrup An excellent addition
to coffee drinks and desserts.

- ¼ cup (50g) superfine sugar
- 1¼ cups (300ml) water
- ¾ cup (125g) semi-sweet chocolate, chopped

Heat the sugar and water gently in a saucepan until dissolved. Boil for 1 minute, then take the saucepan off the heat and stir in the chocolate until melted. Reheat to make a shiny syrup.

Ice Cubes for Coffee

The joy of drinking iced coffee is diminished when the ice melts and dilutes the drink. These ice cubes are easy to make and store and will ensure that you have a delicious drink right to the last sip.

Brewed coffee ice cubes

Brew coffee using your chosen method (see page 20). Allow it to cool to room temperature then pour into a silicone ice-cube tray. Freeze for 3–4 hours, then transfer the cubes to a freezer bag and store in the freezer.

Mocha ice cubes

Make ⅔ cup (150ml) of cold-brew coffee (see page 46), then mix with 1 dessertspoon of Chocolate Syrup (see page 105), and 1 cup (250ml) of milk or oat milk. Pour into a silicone ice-cube tray. Freeze overnight, then transfer the cubes to a freezer bag and store in the freezer. These ice cubes are delicious in iced or cold-brew coffee and milkshakes.

Maple coffee ice cubes

Brew coffee using your chosen method (see page 20) and sweeten to taste with maple syrup. Stir well, then allow to cool to room temperature and pour into a silicone ice-cube tray. Freeze for 3–4 hours, then transfer the cubes to a freezer bag and store in the freezer.

Vanilla ice cubes

Place 1 cup (250ml) of milk or oat milk, ⅔ cup (150ml) of condensed milk, 2 teaspoons of superfine sugar, and 1½ teaspoons of vanilla essence in a milk pan on the stovetop. Warm gently to mix and dissolve the sugar, then allow to cool to room temperature and pour into a silicone ice-cube tray. Freeze overnight, then transfer the cubes to a freezer bag and store in the freezer. Delicious in iced or cold-brew coffee.

Caramel ice cubes

Place 1 cup (250ml) of almond milk, ⅔ cup (150ml) of condensed milk, 2 teaspoons of brown sugar, and 2 teaspoons of caramel syrup in a milk pan on the stovetop. Warm gently to mix and dissolve the sugar, then allow to cool to room temperature and pour into a silicone ice-cube tray. Freeze overnight, then transfer the cubes to a freezer bag and store in the freezer. Delicious in iced or cold-brew coffee.

Minty ice cubes

Place a handful of chopped mint leaves with 2 teaspoons of vanilla essence and 1 dessertspoon of superfine sugar in a pitcher. Add 1¼ cups (300ml) of slightly cooled boiled water and stir to dissolve the sugar. Allow the mixture to cool to room temperature then sieve and pour into a silicone ice-cube tray. Freeze for 3–4 hours, then transfer the cubes to a freezer bag and store in the freezer. Perfect in cold-brew coffee.

Coffee Granita
An impressive dinner-party dessert that is easy to make in advance.

SERVES 6

- 2 cups (500ml) strong-brewed coffee, hot
- 1 teaspoon brown sugar
- ⅓ cup + 2 tablespoons (100ml) dark coffee liqueur
- half and half, to serve
- grated chocolate, to serve

In a large pitcher, mix the hot coffee and sugar, stirring well until dissolved. Allow the coffee to cool, then add the liqueur. Once fully cooled, add the mixture to a shallow ice-cream container and freeze for 1 hour, or until starting to become slushy. Use a fork to mix up the ice crystals then freeze for a further 20–30 minutes, repeating the process until you have the desired texture. Serve in glass bowls with a splash of half and half and some grated chocolate.

Espresso Slush
Simple and refreshing, this drink can be served with a slice of lemon.

MAKES 1 DRINK

- 2 shots espresso, sweetened to taste and cooled
- 5-6 ice cubes
- slice of lemon, to serve

Put the espresso in a blender and add the ice cubes one at a time, blitzing after each until you have a slushy texture. Pour into a glass and serve with a slice of lemon.

Affogato

The Italian word *affogato* means "drowned" in English. Drown a scoop of vanilla gelato in a shot of espresso for a creamy, sharp, and sweet dessert. It's the perfect ending to a meal—especially if you can't decide whether you want dessert or coffee!

Variations

- Add some crumbled amaretti cookies or biscotti to the ice cream.
- Add a splash of liqueur to the coffee— try grappa, Drambuie, or brandy.

Coffee Ice Cream

An easy, make-at-home version of a favorite dessert.

MAKES ABOUT 2½ CUPS (600ML)

- 1 x 14 ounce (397g) can condensed milk
- ⅔ cup (150ml) strong-brewed coffee
- 1¼ cups (300ml) heavy cream
- melted chocolate, for drizzling

Mix the condensed milk with the coffee and chill in the refrigerator. Whip the cream until thick then fold into the chilled coffee. Freeze in a sealed ice-cream container for about 6 hours. Give it a really good stir after a couple of hours to break up the ice crystals, then return to the freezer. Serve the ice cream drizzled with melted chocolate.

Minty Coffee Popsicles
Mint adds a refreshing twist to this creamy frozen coffee treat.

MAKES 6

– 1 large handful chopped mint leaves
– 2 cups (450ml) strong-brewed coffee
– ½ cup (120ml) condensed milk

You will also need:
– popsicle molds

Place the mint leaves in a heat-safe bowl and pour the hot coffee over them. Stir well and allow to steep for approximately 30–60 minutes. Strain the coffee into a pitcher and add the condensed milk. Stir well to combine, then pour into popsicle molds, leaving room at the top for the popsicles to expand. Freeze for about 6 hours, or until fully frozen. Remove the popsicles from the molds and serve immediately.

Coffee and Caramel Popsicles

Serve as a sweet, rich, and decadent dessert.

MAKES 8

- 2 cups (450ml) strong-brewed coffee
- ½ cup (120ml) oat milk
- 3 tablespoons caramel syrup
- 1 level tablespoon brown sugar

You will also need:
- popsicle molds

Place all the ingredients in a small saucepan and gently warm to dissolve the sugar. Stir well, then allow the mixture to cool. Pour into popsicle molds, leaving room at the top for the popsicles to expand. Freeze for about 6 hours, or until fully frozen. Remove the popsicles from the molds and serve immediately.

Coconut and Coffee Popsicles

Delicious summer flavors for a hot day.

MAKES 4

- 1 cup (225ml) strong-brewed coffee
- ½ cup (120ml) plant-based coconut milk
- ½ tablespoon brown sugar
- melted chocolate, cooled, to drizzle

You will also need:
- popsicle molds

In a large pitcher, mix the coffee, milk, and sugar, stirring until the sugar has dissolved. Allow the mixture to cool. Pour into popsicle molds, leaving room at the top for the popsicles to expand. Freeze for about 6 hours, or until fully frozen. Remove the popsicles from the molds and use a fork to drizzle chocolate over them before serving.

Tipsy Orange and Coffee Popsicles

Perfect to enjoy when the weather is hot, with a little alcoholic kick that makes them a hit at parties.

MAKES 6

- 2 cups (450ml) strong-brewed coffee
- 2 measures orange liqueur
- 1 tablespoon brown sugar
- zest of 1 orange, finely grated

You will also need:

- popsicle molds

In a large pitcher, mix the coffee, orange liqueur, sugar, and zest, stirring until the sugar has dissolved. Allow the mixture to cool. Pour into popsicle molds, leaving some room at the top for the popsicles to expand. Freeze for about 6 hours, or until fully frozen. Remove the popsicles from the molds and serve immediately.

Spicy

Coffee pairs perfectly with sweet things, but it can also be an unusual complement to steaks, ribs, chili, and more. Rub it on and mix it in to take savory dishes to a whole new level, then see if your family and friends can guess the secret ingredient!

Coffee Steak

Take four room-temperature steaks, drizzle with olive oil, season with plenty of salt and pepper, then sprinkle them with freshly ground coffee, followed by brown sugar. Turn the steaks over and repeat. Cook in a pan on a high heat, or on the barbecue, to create a crust. Cook for about 6 minutes, turning every minute for medium rare. Cook for longer if you like your steak well done. Serve with green vegetables. Serves 4.

Cod with Coffee-Buttered Noodles

A simple, quick, and impressive dinner for two.

SERVES 2

For the cod:
- 2 x cod loins
- olive oil spray
- 1 lemon, halved
- cayenne pepper

For the noodles:
- 2 cups (300g) thin rice noodles
- 1½ tablespoons salted butter
- 3 tablespoons brewed coffee
- 2 tablespoons soy sauce
- chopped scallions and cilantro, to garnish
- steamed green beans, to serve

Preheat the oven to 350°F. Place the cod loins on a cookie sheet lined with aluminum foil, spray with the olive oil, squeeze half a lemon over each loin, then sprinkle with cayenne pepper. Bake the fish in the oven for 20 minutes, or until cooked through.

While the fish is cooking, cook the noodles according to packet instructions and drain. Add the butter, coffee, and soy sauce to the hot noodles and gently stir through. Garnish the noodles with the scallions and cilantro and serve with the fish and green beans.

One-Pan Coffee-Roasted Vegetables

Preheat the oven to 350°F. Chop three carrots and three parsnips in half lengthwise and lay out in a roasting pan. Mix 2 tablespoons of olive oil with 1 teaspoon of instant coffee powder, a ½ teaspoon of salt, and a ½ teaspoon of brown sugar. Pour the oil mixture over the veggies and toss to make sure they are fully covered. Season with salt and pepper and sprinkle with sesame seeds (optional). Roast for about 30 minutes or until soft and browned. Serves 4.

Maple and Coffee Ribs with
BBQ Sauce Coffee adds a counterpoint
to the sweetness of maple syrup.

SERVES 4

- 2 racks of pre-prepared
  pork ribs
- olive oil, for drizzling
- salt and pepper, to season

For the BBQ sauce:
- 8 tablespoons tomato
  ketchup
- 4 tablespoons
  balsamic vinegar
- 4 tablespoons maple syrup
- 1 tablespoon instant
  espresso powder
- 1 teaspoon paprika
- salt and pepper, to taste

You will also need:
- roasting pan
- aluminum foil

Preheat the oven to 350°F. Drizzle the ribs with olive oil and season with salt and pepper. Place in a roasting pan and cover with aluminum foil. Cook for 1 hour, then remove the foil and cook for a further 30 minutes. Warm all the sauce ingredients together in a small saucepan on the stovetop. When the sauce comes to a simmer, reduce the heat and whisk to thicken. Serve the ribs drizzled with the sauce.

Crispy Coffee Tofu
This soft-on-the-inside, crispy-on-the-outside tofu soaks up a delicious combination of flavors.

- 2 cups (500g) firm tofu, drained
- 2 tablespoons cornmeal, for dusting
- salt and pepper, to taste
- sesame oil, for frying

For the sauce:
- 1 shot espresso
- 2 tablespoons light soy sauce
- 2 tablespoons Chinese vinegar
- 2 tablespoons oyster sauce
- 2 tablespoons runny honey

To serve:
- cooked rice
- 2 scallions, chopped
- handful of cilantro leaves, chopped

Preheat the oven on low heat. Cut the tofu into large strips, dust with the cornmeal, and season with salt and pepper. Heat the sesame oil in a wok and fry the tofu until golden—about 3-5 minutes on each side. Keep the tofu warm in the oven while you make the sauce. Warm all the sauce ingredients together in a saucepan on the stovetop. Bring the sauce to a simmer, then turn the heat down low. Serve the tofu with rice, drizzled with the sauce and garnished with scallions and cilantro.

Mocha Chili A classic chili recipe, with some unusual ingredients.

SERVES 4

– 1 tablespoon olive oil
– 1 large onion, chopped
– 2 garlic cloves, minced
– 1 small or medium fresh red chili, seeds removed and finely chopped
– 2¼ cups (500g) ground beef
– 2 x 14 ounce (400g) cans of chopped tomatoes
– 1 teaspoon instant espresso powder
– 1 tablespoon tomato paste
– 1½ tablespoons semi-sweet chocolate, chopped
– ½ teaspoon sugar
– 1 beef bouillon cube, crumbled
– 1 x 14 ounce (400g) can of black beans, rinsed
– chili flakes, to taste (optional)
– salt and pepper, to taste

To serve:
– tortillas
– grated cheese
– sour cream
– guacamole

Heat the oil in a large pan. Add the onion, garlic, and chili and cook until browned slightly and softened. Add the beef, breaking it up with a spoon, and continue to cook until the meat is browned. Add the tomatoes, espresso powder, and tomato paste and cook over low heat for about 20 minutes. Add the chocolate, sugar, bouillon cube, and beans and stir well, then cook for a further 15 minutes over low heat. Add a small sprinkle of chili flakes, if desired, and season to taste with salt and pepper. Serve with tortillas, grated cheese, sour cream, and guacamole.

PERFECT COFFEE PAIRINGS

You will have your own favorite things to eat with a cup of coffee, but if you're looking for inspiration, here are some delicious suggestions for different times of day.

BREAKFAST

Scrambled eggs, omelets, eggs on toast
Crepes and pancakes
Peanut butter and jelly on toast
French toast
Banana on toast
Oatmeal with berries and maple syrup
Bacon

MID-MORNING AND AFTERNOON TEA

Brownies and chocolate cake
Fruit cakes and scones
Panettone
Sweet pastries

LUNCH

Charcuterie
Cheese board
Grilled cheese sandwiches
Smoked salmon and cream cheese bagel
Cheese on toast
Berry fruit salad

DINNER AND AFTER DINNER

Curry
Steak
Biscotti and amaretti cookies
Turkish delight
Mint chocolate and salted
caramel chocolate

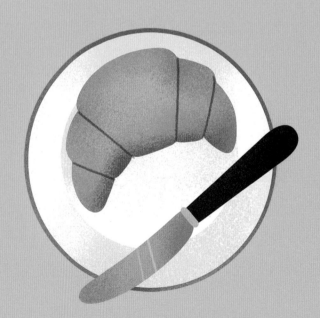

Index

Acknowledgments

With thanks to Dan at Blueprint Coffee and Books, Whitstable, for gifting delicious house-roasted coffee.

About the Author & Illustrator

Sarah Ford has written many giftable bestsellers, including *50 Ways to Kill a Slug*, *What Would Unicorn Do?*, *Be a Flamingo*, *The Chinese Zodiac,* and *It's the Little Things*.

Clare Owen is a freelance illustrator and designer currently based in Bristol, UK. Her clients include *Elle* France, *O: The Oprah Magazine,* Chronicle Books, Penguin Random House, Quarto, Hallmark US, Marks and Spencer, and Airbnb.